D1624874

THE GREAT OUTDOORS

Fly Fishing

By Ellen Hopkins

Consultant:
Education Committee
Federation of Fly Fishers

CAPSTONE
HIGH-INTEREST
BOOKS

an imprint of Capstone Press
Mankato, Minnesota

Capstone High-Interest Books are published by Capstone Press
151 Good Counsel Drive, P.O. Box 669, Mankato, Minnesota 56002
http://www.capstone-press.com

Library of Congress Cataloging-in-Publication Data
Hopkins, Ellen.
   Fly Fishing/by Ellen Hopkins.
   p. cm.—(The great outdoors)
   Includes bibliographical references and an index (p. 48).
   ISBN 0-7368-0914-7
   1. Fly fishing—Juvenile literature. [1. Fly fishing. 2. Fishing.] I. Title. II. Series.
SH456 .H67 2002
799.1'24—dc21   00-012552

Summary: Describes the equipment, skills, conservation issues, and safety concerns of fly fishing.

Editorial Credits
Carrie Braulick, editor; Lois Wallentine, product planning editor; Timothy Halldin,
   cover designer and illustrator; Katy Kudela, photo researcher

Photo Credits
Bob Pool/TOM STACK & ASSOCIATES, 6, 21
Capstone Press/Gary Sundermeyer, cover (bottom left, bottom right), 4, 9 (foreground),
   13, 14, 17, 18 (foreground), 28, 38
Comstock, Inc., 1, 9 (background), 18 (background)
Jeff Fooh/TOM STACK & ASSOCIATES, 10
Jeff Henry/Roche Jaune Pictures, Inc., 44
Loren Irving/Gnass Photo Images, 35
Photo Network, 24; Photo Network/Nancy Hoyt Belcher, cover (top right), B. Dodge,
   22; Stephen Saks, 30
Photri-Microstock, 36
Rob and Ann Simpson, 40 (bottom), 41 (bottom)
Unicorn Stock Photos/Joe Sohm, 33
Visuals Unlimited, 40 (top); Visuals Unlimited/Bernd Wittich, 42 (bottom)
William H. Mullins, 41 (top), 42 (top)

1 2 3 4 5 6 07 06 05 04 03 02

Table of Contents

CHAPTER 1

Fly Fishing

Modern fly fishers use rods that are specially made for fly fishing. They also use reels and line. They tie flies made of manufactured materials to their line. These flies are attached to a hook. Flies may look like insects or animals that fish eat. Fly fishers cast the line into the water. They hope a fish will try to eat the fly and become hooked.

History of Fly Fishing

People fished to survive in prehistoric times. They sometimes used darts, spears, or nets. They also used small pointed pieces of wood, bone, or stone called gorges. They covered the gorges with bait and attached them

People have been fly fishing for thousands of years.

Fly fishers often fish in streams and rivers.

to a line. They may have attached the line to a rod made of wood. A gorge stuck in a fish's throat after the fish swallowed it. People then used the line or rod to bring the fish out of the water.

Some historians believe fly fishing began in the area that is now Macedonia. This country is located in southeastern Europe. A book from about A.D. 200 explains how

Macedonians made flies out of wool and feathers. They cast the flies into the water to catch fish.

In later years, fishing was no longer necessary for people's survival. But people still fished to add variety to their diets and for recreation. Today, fly fishing is a popular North American sport. People fly fish with a large variety of flies made of materials such as animal hair, feathers, and cork.

Common Fish

Fly fishers in North America fish for a variety of fish species. All animals within a species share certain physical features.

Many North American fish live in freshwater. These areas include streams, rivers, ponds, and lakes. Freshwater has little salt in it. Other fish live in salt water. These fish live in seas and oceans.

North American fly fishers often fish for bass and trout. These fish usually live in freshwater streams and rivers. They sometimes live in lakes.

Fly fishers also may fish for crappies, perch, and sunfish. These small freshwater fish are called panfish.

Some fly fishers fish for salmon. North American salmon include Atlantic and Pacific salmon. Fly fishers often fish for Atlantic salmon in northeastern Canada. They fish for Atlantic landlocked salmon in lakes in the northeastern United States and eastern Canada. These salmon live in bodies of water that are surrounded by land areas. Fly fishers often fish for Pacific salmon on the northwestern coast of the United States.

Atlantic and Pacific salmon that live in salt water travel to freshwater rivers and large streams to spawn. Fish lay eggs when they spawn.

Fly fishers may fish for saltwater fish such as permit, mackerel, bonefish, and barracuda. Other popular saltwater fish include blue fish, shad, and tuna. Most saltwater fly fishers use special equipment to catch large fish. Some saltwater fish weigh more than 50 pounds (23 kilograms).

Foil-Wrapped Trout

Ingredients:
1 tomato
1 medium onion
1 lemon
1 trout fillet (boneless)
1 teaspoon lemon juice
Salt and pepper, as desired
2 1/2 teaspoons chopped
   garlic, or as desired

Equipment:
Sharp knife
Aluminum foil
Metal spatula

1. Cut tomato and onion into thin slices.

2. Cut lemon into wedges.

3. Place fish fillet on a large piece of aluminum foil.

4. Sprinkle fish with lemon juice and salt and pepper.

5. Add slices of tomato, onion, and chopped garlic.

6. Fold the foil tightly around the fish and cook on a grill,
over a campfire, or in an oven preheated to 325 degrees
Fahrenheit (160 degrees Celsius). Turn the fish over with a
metal spatula after about 10 minutes. A fish fillet that is
about 12 inches (30 centimeters) long usually is fully cooked
after about 20 minutes. Fish is fully cooked when it is hot in
the center. Serve with lemon wedges.

Serves: 1   Children should have adult supervision.

CHAPTER 2

Equipment

In North America, most freshwater fishers attach live bait or lures to their fishing line. Lures are wood, metal, or plastic objects people use to attract fish. But fly fishers attach flies to their line. Many fly fishers purchase flies. But some people make their own flies. Fly fishers also use specially made rods, reels, and line for their sport.

Fly Rods

Fly fishers use fly rods to cast flies. Most fly rods are made of a strong, lightweight material called graphite. Fly fishers usually use rods that are about 8.5 to 9 feet (2.6 to 2.7 meters) long.

Fly fishers use rods to cast flies.

Each fly rod bends in a certain way. This movement is called action. A fly rod's action can be slow, medium, or fast. Slow-action rods usually are easiest to cast. Fast-action rods allow fly fishers to cast longer distances than slow- or medium-action rods.

Fly Reels

Fly rods have reels to hold line. Most reels are made of a lightweight metal called aluminum. Some reels are made of graphite.

People use reels to help them bring in hooked fish. Hooked fish usually run with the line. Fly fishers place the middle finger of the hand that holds the rod over the line. This action stops the run. Fly fishers then reel in any slack in the line as the fish moves. The fish gradually comes closer as the reel's spool collects line.

Most fly fishers use single-action reels. These reels turn once with each crank of the handle. Other fly fishers use multiplier reels. One crank of the handle turns these reels one and one-half to two times. Multiplier reels are helpful when hooked fish swim long distances with the line.

Most fly fishers use single-action reels.

Most fly reels have a drag system. This system includes a device located on the reel's spool or cover. Drag systems slow down the line as it goes out. They help fly fishers control the line. Fly fishers can adjust some drag systems.

Fly Line
Fly fishing line is called fly line. It is made of a combination of materials such as Dacron and

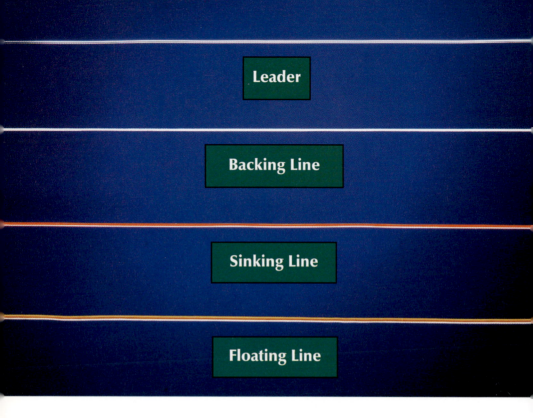

Leader

Backing Line

Sinking Line

Floating Line

vinyl. Dacron is a manufactured fiber. Most fly
lines are 90 feet (27 meters) long. Fly line is
thicker and heavier than other fishing line. In
bait and lure fishing, the weight of the bait or
lure helps pull line off the reel during a cast.
But lightweight flies cannot pull line off the
reel. The heavy fly line helps fly fishers cast.

Fly line comes in different weights. No. 1
fly line is the lightest. The heaviest fly line is
No. 12. Most fly fishers use line weights

between No. 4 and No. 8 for average freshwater conditions.

Fly line either floats or sinks. Sinking line usually sinks more than 2 feet (.6 meter) below the surface. Some fly line is intermediate. This fly line sinks to about 1 foot (.3 meter) below the surface.

Backing Line and Leaders

Fly fishers put backing line on their reel before the fly line. They attach one end of this braided Dacron line to the reel. They attach the other end to the fly line. Fly fishers may put 25 to 500 feet (7.6 to 152 meters) of backing line on the reel. Backing line allows fly fishers to give a running fish more line. Large fish often run long distances. These fish can break the line if there is not enough of it.

Fly fishers tie a 1- to 30-foot (.3- to 9.1-meter) nylon leader to the other end of the fly line. Leaders usually are made of thin monofilament line. This line is made of a single nylon strand. It is almost invisible to fish.

Most leaders are tapered. The thick end attaches to the fly line. This part is called the butt. The middle part is called the taper. The tip is called the tippet. Tippets usually are 1 to 3 feet (.3 to .9 meter) long. Fly fishers make a knot to tie the fly to the tippet.

Flies

Fly fishers use different fly patterns. Flies may look like insects. They also may look like animals fish eat such as small fish, frogs, or salamanders.

Dry flies are one type of fly pattern. These flies look like insects floating on the water's surface. Fly fishers use floating line with dry flies. They cast dry flies onto the water and let them float for a few seconds to attract fish. They recast if a fish does not take the fly. Fly fishers often cast dry flies upstream.

Fly fishers often use dry flies called bass bugs to fish for bass. These flies can be made of a variety of materials such as wood, cork, foam, plastic, or animal hair.

Wet flies are another type of fly pattern. These flies sink. Fly fishers use sinking line with wet flies. Wet flies may look like living or drowned insects. They also may look like small fish or other animals living in the water.

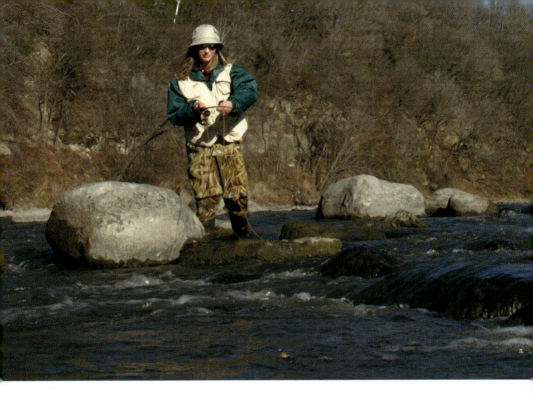

Fly fishers often cast dry flies upstream.

Fly fishers sometimes slowly drag wet flies upstream to make them appear more life-like.

Some wet flies look like nymphs. Nymphs are insects in a stage of development just before they become adults. Nymphs live in the water. Fly fishers may move the line back and forth to imitate the way nymphs move.

Other wet flies are bucktails or streamers. These flies look like minnows or other small fish. Bucktails and streamers have material attached to them called wings. Streamers have

17

Dry Flies

Nymphs

Wet Flies

Streamers & Bucktails

Saltwater Flies

Bass Bugs

Dry Flies
1. Stimulator
2. Elk Hair Caddis
3. Pale Morning Dun
4. Adams
5. Royal Wulff

Nymphs
1. Black Stonefly
2. Gold-ribbed Hare's Ear
3. Pheasant Tail
4. Bead Head Prince Nymph

Wet Flies
1. Wooly Worm
2. Hare's Ear Soft Hackle
3. Royal Coachman
4. Gold-ribbed Hare's Ear
   with wing

Streamers & Bucktails
1. Marabou Muddler
2. Matuka
3. Wooly Bugger
4. Blacknosed Dace

Saltwater Flies
1. Mini Puff
2. Clouser Minnow
3. Imitator Shrimp
4. Lefty's Deceiver

Bass Bugs
1. Messinger Frog
2. Dragonfly
3. Diving Frog

wings made of feathers. Bucktails have wings made of animal hair.

Fly fishers sometimes use attractor flies. These flies do not look like a certain insect or animal. Fly fishers use attractor flies both on and under the water's surface.

Some flies are designed to be used in salt water. Many of these flies are streamers. Saltwater flies sometimes look like shrimp, crabs, or minnows.

Hooks

Flies are attached to hooks. The hooks become caught in a fish's mouth and prevent the fish from escaping. Fly fishers should make sure their hooks are sharp. A sharp hook is more likely to stay in a fish's mouth than a dull hook.

Many fly fishers use hooks without barbs. These sharp points extend from behind a fishhook's point. Barbless hooks cause less damage to the fish.

Other Gear

Fly fishers use gear for outdoor protection. They use sunglasses to protect their eyes from the sun. They may use polarized sunglasses.

These sunglasses can help reduce glare on the water. Sunglasses also protect the eyes from stray hooks. Fly fishers may wear a hat with a wide brim to shade their face. Many fly fishers carry insect repellent to prevent insect bites.

Fly fishers sometimes wade into the water to cast. They wear waterproof garments called waders to stay dry in the water. Many fly fishers wear chest waders that cover their legs and upper body. Chest waders have straps that go over the shoulders. Most chest waders have waterproof boots attached to them.

Other fly fishers wear hip boots. These waders cover fly fishers' legs. They have boots attached to them. Hip boots have suspenders that attach to a fisher's belt.

Fly fishers use other equipment. Many fly fishers carry boxes to store their flies. They wear vests with pockets, pouches, and clips. They can use the vests to carry fly boxes, line, leaders, and hooks. Fly fishers may carry clippers to cut line. They may use forceps to remove a hook from a fish's mouth. Fishers can firmly grasp objects with forceps. Many fly fishers bring a flashlight. Fishers may need to leave their fishing areas in the dark. Fish often

Chest waders cover a fly fisher's legs and upper body.

eat just before it becomes dark. Fly fishers also may bring a net to handle a hooked fish.

A thermometer may be useful to fly fishers. Some fish are more likely to bite when the water is at a certain temperature. For example, brown trout prefer temperatures that are between 55 and 65 degrees Fahrenheit (13 to 18 degrees Celsius).

Fly fishers should bring a first aid kit. Fishers can use items in this kit such as gauze and bandages to treat people who become injured.

CHAPTER 3

Skills and Techniques

Fly fishers use various methods to catch fish. Most fly fishers wade into the water to fish or fish from shore. But some fly fishers fish from boats. Fly fishers should learn about the features and habits of the fish that they are trying to catch.

Reading the Water

Skilled fly fishers know where to find fish. This skill is called "reading the water." Lake fish often move to different areas to search for food. River and stream fish often stay in one place and let the current bring food to them. Fly fishers try to find out which way fish are

Fly fishers must learn a variety of skills.

Fly fishers often fish near water edges and plants.

moving. They watch for fish to rise to the water's surface. They look for places where fish are likely to feed. They may fish in a lake's inlet or outlet to a river. Fish often gather in these areas. The water that enters and exits lakes often carries more oxygen and food than other lake areas.

Stream fish often gather in small pools of slow-moving water called pocket water to rest.

Rocks, logs, or other structures in the water create pocket water. These objects slow the current's speed by changing its direction.

Fly fishers look for fish in other places. Fish often spend time near visible lines in the water called edges. A row of plants or an area where calm water meets fast water may form edges. Fish often live near fallen logs, large rocks, or sandbars.

The Approach

Fly fishers carefully approach and wade into the water. Fish have good eyesight. They often become startled when objects move above them. Fly fishers try not to form large or moving shadows over the water. Fly fishers may wear clothing that blends with the surroundings. Some fishing experts believe that bright colors can scare fish away.

Fish can sense vibrations. Fish often sense the vibration of people walking on shore. Fly fishers stay calm and walk into the water slowly. They try not to kick rocks or walk on loose rocks. Large splashes may frighten fish.

Fly fishers should stay still for a few moments after they wade into the water. This pause in movement may help calm any frightened fish.

The Cast

The fly cast has two parts. These parts are the backcast and the forward cast. Fly fishers make the backcast first. They begin with 25 to 30 feet (7.6 to 9.1 meters) of line spread straight out in front of them. Fly fishers grip the rod with their palm facing down. The thumb should lie along the rod's top. Fly fishers keep their wrist tight. They then can pull off some of the line from the reel with their free hand. The amount of line they pull off depends on how far they want to cast.

Fly fishers lift the rod's tip to begin the backcast. They quickly move the rod's tip just past their shoulder. They then stop the

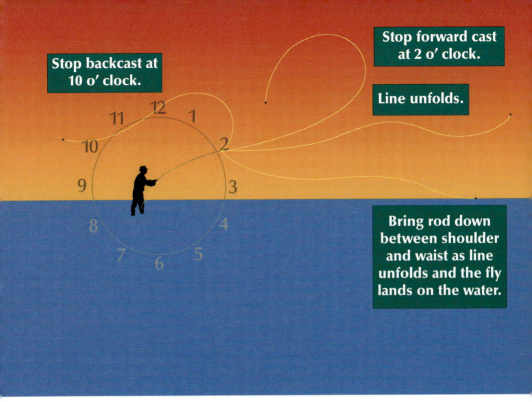

movement without bending the wrist. The line should unfold behind them.

Fly fishers begin the forward cast when the line is almost straight behind them. They quickly move the rod forward. They stop the movement just after the rod passes the shoulder. They then let out some line from their free hand. They move the rod down between their

shoulder and waist as the line straightens out in front of them.

Fly fishers sometimes false cast. Fly fishers move quickly from the backcast to the forward cast when they false cast. They keep the line above the water's surface.

People false cast for various reasons. It helps the line slip easily from the reel to the distance needed for the cast. It also can dry out a fly or help fly fishers learn the casting movement.

Fly fishers may false cast before they begin fishing.

CHAPTER 4

Conservation

Fish populations are not as large as they once were. Many of the water sources where trout once lived have been polluted or destroyed. Trout can only live in about 15 percent of the waters they once lived in. More than 80 fish species are in danger of dying out.

Fly fishers can protect fish populations and their habitats. These are the natural conditions and places in which fish live. Fly fishers should follow the state or province fishing rules. They also should take any trash home with them or place it in trash cans.

Fly fishers can help preserve the areas in which they fish.

Conservation Efforts

In 1940, the U.S. government established the U.S. Fish and Wildlife Service. This department restores fish populations and damaged habitats. It also establishes wildlife refuges. Fish, birds, and other animals live in these protected areas.

The U.S. Fish and Wildlife Service oversees the National Fish Hatchery System (NFHS). The NFHS raises fish in hatcheries. These fish are released into water sources to help increase the populations of certain fish.

Fisheries and Oceans Canada (DFO) helps protect and maintain fish habitats in Canada. DFO also maintains fish populations and conducts studies on how climate and other factors affect fish habitats.

Other groups work to restore water sources and fish populations. These groups include the Federation of Fly Fishers, Trout Unlimited, and the Native Fish Conservancy. Members of these groups sometimes rebuild gravel beds where fish spawn. Some groups build buffer strips. These strips of land prevent pollutants from entering water sources.

Fish raised in hatcheries can help increase populations of certain fish species.

Fly fishers should release fish that they do not plan to eat. They should release the fish as soon as they remove the hook. They try to keep the fish in the water. Fish quickly run out of oxygen when they are removed from the water.

Fly fishers follow certain steps to release fish. They hold fish underwater for a few seconds to allow them to receive oxygen through their gills. Fish breathe through these openings on their sides. Fly fishers should make sure fish are facing upstream. Fish that are not facing upstream may be carried upside down by the current. They may die because they are unable to flip over.

Licenses and Regulations
Fly fishers need to follow government rules. These rules help protect fish populations. States and provinces require fishers to have a fishing license at a certain age. This age ranges from 12 to 16.

Most people buy full-season licenses. These licenses allow fly fishers to fish in their home state or province throughout the year or fishing season. States and provinces allow fishing during fishing seasons. The length of seasons varies according to the location and fish species. Fly fishers usually need to buy separate licenses or permits when they fish outside of their home state or province.

Fly fishers should release fish that they do not plan to eat.

Fly fishers also must follow limit regulations. These rules allow one person to catch a certain number of fish in one day. Limit rules vary by area and fish species. Some states and provinces close rivers to fishing during spawning season.

CHAPTER 5

Safety

All water areas can be dangerous. Fly fishers must follow safety guidelines. These fishers reduce their chances of injury. They also are prepared if accidents do occur.

Water Safety

Fly fishers should be careful when they wade into the water. Rocks often are slippery. Currents can be strong. Fly fishers should walk sideways into the current. They should try to avoid deep water and fast-moving shallow water.

Fly fishers in boats should wear life jackets. Life jackets can help fishers survive if their boat tips or if they fall out of the boat.

Fly fishers in boats must wear life jackets.

Fly fishers should carefully wade into the water.

Weather Safety

Fly fishers should learn the day's weather forecast before they go out to fish. They should watch for approaching thunderstorms as they fish. Fly fishers who are caught in storms should quickly get out of the water. They also should stay away from tall trees and ridges. Lightning is more likely to strike these places. Fly fishers should lay down their rods during storms. Graphite fly rods can attract lightning.

Fly fishers should try to stay warm in cold weather. They should add layers of clothing if they become cold. Fly fishers may get hypothermia if they become too cold. This condition occurs when a person's body temperature drops below 95 degrees Fahrenheit (35 degrees Celsius). People who get hypothermia can become confused and tired. They may even die.

Other Safety Guidelines

Safe fly fishers are careful around others. They look around to make sure no one is nearby when they cast. Beginning fly fishers should fish with another person. Other people can help if an accident occurs.

Fly fishers should know how to use the items in their first aid kits. They then can treat small injuries.

Safe fly fishers take their sport seriously. They are aware of their surroundings and are prepared for accidents. These fly fishers set a good example for other participants in the sport.

Tarpon

Tarpon live off the southeastern coast of the United States in the Atlantic Ocean and the Caribbean Sea. They are common off Florida's coast. People usually try to catch these fish for recreation. Tarpon are not considered edible in the United States.

Description: Tarpon have dark blue to green backs that fade into silver along the fish's sides. They have large scales. Tarpon usually weigh about 45 pounds (20 kilograms). But tarpon can weigh more than 100 pounds (45 kilograms).

Habitat: near river mouths and inlets, bays, offshore waters; young tarpon may live in freshwater

Food: young fish, crabs, shrimp

Flies: Cockroach, Seducer, Purple People Eater, Boca Grande, Homosassa Special, Golden Claw

Permit

People often fly fish for permit off Florida's coast. Many experienced fly fishers enjoy the challenge of fishing for permit. Many fly fishers believe permit are easily frightened.

Description: Permit have silver sides and blue backs. They have large eyes and large, deeply forked tails. Permit usually weigh about 20 pounds (9 kilograms).

Habitat: shallow water along level ground, channels

Food: shrimp, crabs

Flies: Merkin's Crab, Snapping Shrimp, Ghost Shrimp

Smallmouth Bass

Smallmouth bass are common in North American freshwater. These fish are strong for their size. Smallmouth bass are known for their leaping and fighting abilities.

Description: Smallmouth bass are green-brown to brown. They have a mouth that extends to the front of the eye. They have dark, broken vertical bands along their sides. Smallmouth bass usually weigh about .5 to 4 pounds (.2 to 1.8 kilograms).

Habitat: deep, cool lakes; rocky, quickly flowing streams

Food: minnows, insects, crawfish, frogs

Flies: nymphs; streamers such as the Wooly Bugger, Marabou Leech, Black Marabou Muddler, and Muddler Minnow

Bluegill

Bluegill are common throughout North America. They are a popular type of panfish.

Description: Bluegill are olive to bronze. They have about six dark vertical bars on their sides. They have a large black spot on the back edge of the gill cover. They also have a black spot at the edge of their dorsal fin. This fin is located on top of a fish's back near its tail. Bluegill usually weigh about .3 to .8 pound (.1 to .4 kilogram).

Habitat: warm lakes, ponds, slow-moving streams and rivers with sandy bottoms; weedy areas, near structures, shallow water near shore

Food: insects, plants, fish eggs, small fish, snails

Flies: dry flies such as poppers and sponge spiders; nymphs such as the Muskrat and Gold-ribbed Hare's Ear; streamers such as the Mickey Finn and Marabou Muddler

Rainbow Trout

Rainbow trout live throughout North America. Some of these fish live in the Great Lakes area near Michigan. They are common in the northwestern areas of North America. Rainbow trout are known for their leaping abilities.

Description: Rainbow trout have silver skin covered with small black spots. A pink-orange band usually runs lengthwise along their sides. Rainbow trout usually weigh about 2 pounds (.9 kilogram).

Habitat: cold, quickly flowing rivers and streams; cold lakes

Food: insects, small fish, fish eggs

Flies: nymphs; dry flies such as the Blue-winged Olive, Royal Wulff, Gray Hackle, and Adams

Atlantic Salmon

North American fly fishers can fish for Atlantic salmon off the eastern coast of the United States. They also may fish for Atlantic salmon in rivers and streams of eastern Canada during spawning season.

Description: Atlantic salmon have silver sides with black spots. They have four or fewer spots on their gill cover. Atlantic salmon usually weigh about 8 to 12 pounds (3.6 to 5.4 kilograms).

Habitat: deep pools of water near rocks and other structures; freshwater streams and rivers during spawning season

Food: small fish

Flies: wet flies such as Thunder and Lightning and Jock Scott; dry flies such as the Royal Wulff

Words to Know

buffer strip (BUH-fur STRIP)—a strip of land covered with grass and trees that is designed to catch pollutants

graphite (GRAF-ite)—a common black or gray mineral; fly fishing rods often are made of graphite

leader (LEE-duhr)—a length of thin line that fly fishers tie to their flies

monofilament line (mah-nuh-FI-luh-ment LYNE)—fishing line made of a single thin strand

nymph (NIMF)—a young form of an insect that changes into an adult by repeatedly shedding its skin

spawn (SPAWN)—to lay eggs

taper (TAY-pur)—to become more narrow on one end

tippet (TI-pet)—the thin end of a tapered leader

To Learn More

Bailey, John. *The Young Fishing Enthusiast.* New York: DK Publishing, 1999.

Kreh, Lefty. *101 Fly Fishing Tips.* New York: Lyons Press, 2000.

Solomon, Dane. *Fishing: Have Fun, Be Smart.* Explore the Outdoors. New York: Rosen Publishing Group, 2000.

You also can learn about fly fishing in magazines such as *American Angler* and *Saltwater Fly Fishing*.

Useful Addresses

American Museum of Fly Fishing
P.O. Box 42
Manchester, VT 05254

Canadian Wildlife Service
Environment Canada
Ottawa, ON K1A 0H3
Canada

Federation of Fly Fishers
P.O. Box 1595
Bozeman, MT 59771

Trout Unlimited
1500 Wilson Boulevard
Suite 310
Arlington, VA 22209

U.S. Fish and Wildlife Service
4401 North Fairfax Drive
Arlington, VA 22203

Internet Sites

Canadian Wildlife Service
http://www.cws-scf.ec.gc.ca/cwshom_e.html

Federation of Fly Fishers
http://www.fedflyfishers.org/indexmst.htm

Fly Fish America Online
http://www.flyfishamerica.com

The Fly Fishing Resource Guide
http://www.flyfish.com

GORP—Fishing
http://www.gorp.com/gorp/activity/fishing.htm

Trout Unlimited
http://www.tu.org

Index